The P awa

Alina Arkins
Photographs by Len Doel

REED

CONTENTS

Introduction

Most New Zealanders are able to recognise the pohutukawa, one of our best-known trees. Its habit of flowering during a relatively short period around Christmas time has earned it the name 'New Zealand Christmas Tree'. The characteristic red flowers and massive, twisting trunks, branches and roots are a familiar sight in many of our coastal areas, and often remind us of long summer days at the beach. Many drawings and paintings have been inspired by the form and colour of pohutukawa trees.

As well as being fascinating to look at, especially when flowering, pohutukawa are very well-adapted to the harsh environment they live in. They possess a number of adaptations that help them to cope with the difficult conditions often present in coastal areas, such as strong, salty winds, poor soils and drought.

Pohutukawa flowers produce a large amount of nectar, which attracts birds, insects, lizards and bats. Unfortunately, they also attract the brush-tailed possum. The possum eats the leaves of the tree, sometimes consuming so many leaves that the tree dies.

Although pohutukawa is a coastal plant, its stunning flower display and hardiness has made it a popular tree for planting along streets and in parks and reserves.

Maori uses for pohutukawa

The pohutukawa has special significance for Maori. Some legends tell the story of Tawhaki, who tried to reach the skies. However, Tawhaki fell and died, and it is said that his blood colours the flowers of the pohutukawa. At Cape Reinga, a small pohutukawa tree clings to the northernmost point of New Zealand. The tree is very sacred, as it is thought to mark the entrance that spirits must use to pass on to the next world. Parts of the pohutukawa were also used by Maori for various purposes, for example, the bark for medicinal uses and the wood for making tools and weapons.

Pohutukawa forest once covered large areas of coastal land. Today, however, only small stands of trees remain in most areas.

Gnarled roots of a pohutukawa tree.

Pohutukawa family tree

The pohutukawa is a member of a large family of plants called Myrtaceae, or myrtles. Members of this family are found in many other countries, mostly in the southern hemisphere. There are about 3000 myrtle species.

Some members of the family, such as feijoa and guava, bear edible fruits. Others, including the pohutukawa and the eucalypts (gum trees) of Australia, produce a dry seed capsule that contains hundreds of tiny seeds. Our native manuka and kanuka trees also fall into this category.

The flowers on this feijoa tree look similar to those on a pohutukawa tree.

There are about 60 *Metrosideros* species found in Australia, New Guinea, New Caledonia, New Zealand, the Philippines, and some Pacific islands.

Twelve of these species are endemic to New Zealand. This means that they grow naturally nowhere else in the world. They include the pohutukawa, the rata trees and vines, and the Kermadec Islands pohutukawa (*Metrosideros kermadecensis*). While pohutukawa grow mostly in northern coastal areas, the rata species are found inland throughout our forests.

The bushy Kermadec Islands pohutukawa.

As its name suggests, the Kermadec Islands pohutukawa grows naturally only on the Kermadec Islands, which lie to the north of New Zealand in the subtropical zone. However, this species is commonly planted in towns and cities on mainland New Zealand. It is used because it does not grow to such a large size as *Metrosideros excelsa* (which can cause problems in small gardens!) and it often produces flowers at intervals throughout the year.

Scientific names explained!

Scientists classify living things according to how closely related they are to one another. As well as a common name (such as 'pohutukawa'), every living thing also has a unique scientific name. This is made up of a genus name, which comes first, and a species name, which comes second. Closely related species will often have the same genus name.

The classification of pohutukawa looks like this:

Kingdom: Plantae (all plants)

↘ Division: Angiospermae (flowering plants)

↘ Family: Myrtaceae (myrtles)

↘ Genus: *Metrosideros*

↘ Species: *excelsa*

So, the scientific name of pohutukawa is *Metrosideros excelsa*. It belongs to the family Myrtaceae, which is a subgroup of the Angiospermae division.

Kermadec Islands pohutukawa in flower.

The karo is often mistaken for pohutukawa because its leaves resemble the pohutukawa's and it is also found in coastal areas. However, karo is not closely related to pohutukawa: it belongs to the Pittosporum plant family.

The leaves and seed capsule of the karo tree.

There are three species of rata tree: northern rata (*Metrosideros robusta*), southern rata (*Metrosideros umbellata*), and Bartlett's rata (*Metrosideros bartlettii*). Northern and southern rata produce crimson flowers very similar to those of the pohutukawa. Northern rata grows in forests throughout the North Island and in the northwest of the South Island. Southern rata is found mostly in the South Island, especially on the west coast.

Flowers of Metrosideros fulgens, *a climbing rata.*

A white-flowered climbing rata.

Bartlett's rata has white flowers, and is very rare. It is only found in a few small forest remnants near Cape Reinga, in the Far North.

Northwest Nelson rata (*Metrosideros parkinsonii*) is a smaller tree or shrub, which occurs in the northwest of the South Island, and on Great Barrier and Little Barrier islands.

As well as the three rata tree species, there are six climbing rata species. These grow as vines over other vegetation, and have either white, orange-red, or scarlet flowers.

The northern rata often gets an unusual start in life. It can grow from a seed in the ground, but more usually germinates high up in the branches of another tree. As it grows, it sends its roots down and around the host tree's trunk. Eventually the rata becomes a large tree itself. As the host tree rots away, a cavity is left inside the trunk of the rata. Northern rata may grow as high as 25 metres or more, making it one of New Zealand's tallest flowering trees.

The roots of this northern rata now support it as its trunk — the hole in the middle is where the host tree once stood.

Where do pohutukawa grow?

Pohutukawa are adapted to coastal environments, and this is where they occur naturally. Their range includes the coast of most of the North Island, especially north of Gisborne on the east coast, and New Plymouth, on the west coast. They also grow on the shores of some central North Island lakes, such as Lake Rotorua.

Some of the oldest and largest pohutukawa can be found on the Coromandel Peninsula, and in the Bay of Plenty. They are also found on many of the northern offshore islands, such as Rangitoto, Great and Little Barrier islands, and the Poor Knights Islands. In fact, islands like these are now the only places where pohutukawa trees remain in such numbers as to form an almost continuous canopy, showing us what mainland pohutukawa forests may have looked like in the past.

Although not a part of their natural range, many pohutukawa have been planted inland in our towns and cities, where they are a familiar sight in gardens, parks, and reserves. Some have also been planted in more southerly areas such as Wellington, Nelson, and Banks Peninsula, where they have grown well.

Street planting of pohutukawa.

A. Arkins

This tree grows on top of a large rock in Whakatane.

Pohutukawa on coastal cliffs.

Pohutukawa in an estuary among mangroves.

Pohutukawa on a sandy beach.

Pohutukawa are planted in many parks and reserves.

Some pohutukawa grow along coastal pasture.

ADAPTATIONS FOR COASTAL LIFE

Coastal environments are harsh for plants. They can be very dry, windy, and salty, with poor soil or almost no soil at all. The pohutukawa, however, has evolved some excellent adaptations to help it live in this type of environment.

The dark green upper surface of mature leaves.

These leaves are at an intermediate stage of growth. They are becoming a darker green and are developing the shiny, tough coating on their upper surfaces.

The upper surface of a mature pohutukawa leaf has a tough waxy coating, which protects the leaf from salt spray, drought, and the glare of strong sunlight. The underside of the leaf is covered with tiny hairs, which help to reduce the amount of water lost from the leaf.

The young stems and leaves at the top are soft and covered with many fine hairs. Compare them with the mature leaves at the bottom of the photograph.

This tree has many clumps of aerial roots hanging from its branches.

Pohutukawa bark is thick and rough. This also protects the tree from drought by preventing excessive water loss.

On some pohutukawa trees you may have noticed the reddish, stringy aerial roots that sometimes grow from the tree's trunk and branches. The tree produces these roots to search out nearby moisture sources. This ability enables pohutukawa to grow in areas where there is very little soil. As the roots grow, they can bind together and stabilise rocks and cliff faces, helping to prevent coastal erosion.

Instead of growing straight up with a tall trunk, a mature pohutukawa tree typically has many large trunks and branches that spread outwards and upwards from ground level. This growth habit helps the tree to withstand strong sea breezes. The branches and roots will often grow along the ground as well, spreading the tree's weight over the sometimes unstable surfaces they grow on.

Pohutukawa often have many trunks and branches, some of which may grow across the ground.

Pohutukawa seeds are very small. This means they can be dispersed over long distances by the wind.

All these adaptations make the pohutukawa a good colonising plant. It is often the first to grow in coastal areas, providing shade and shelter for other plants.

A pohutukawa seedling growing on a vertical cliff face.

Did you know?

Pohutukawa trees may reach a height of 25 metres, and the canopy can spread to around 35 metres across. Plant scientists believe that pohutukawa can probably live up to 1000 years in their natural environment. A tree growing at Te Araroa, in the Bay of Plenty, is thought to be the largest known pohutukawa. It stands at 19.8 metres and has a canopy spread of 38.4 metres.

The scientific name of pohutukawa refers to its wood. The word metrosideros means 'iron wood', and the tree is so named because its timber is very hard and strong. These properties, along with its naturally bent and curved branches, made pohutukawa wood useful in the past for building parts of boats and ships, where an angle or curve was required in the timber.

Pohutukawa is the only New Zealand tree that can colonise bare lava. On volcanic Rangitoto Island in the Hauraki Gulf, pohutukawa seedlings were among the first plants to grow on the lava after it had cooled and solidified. Those seedlings are now mature trees, and they have helped to provide a sheltered habitat for other plants to grow in.

Life cycle and evolution

The spectacular crimson flowers of the pohutukawa give a special character to our northern coastlines and beaches. They also play an important part in the tree's life cycle.

Young flower buds.

Flowers are a plant's reproductive structures. Pohutukawa flowers are hermaphrodites, which means that each flower has both male and female parts. The male parts, called stamens,

Older flower buds.

Flower buds just starting to open.

which stick up and give the flower its fluffy, brush-like appearance, produce pollen. The female parts form a pistil and contain ovules.

An important step in the life cycle of flowering plants is pollination. This happens when pollen is transferred from stamen to pistil. Pohutukawa pollen looks like fine, yellow powder. The individual pollen grains are too small to be seen with the naked eye.

There are two types of pollination. Self-pollination occurs when pollen is transferred from one flower to another on the same tree. Cross-pollination occurs when pollen is transferred to a flower on a different tree.

Pohutukawa flower parts

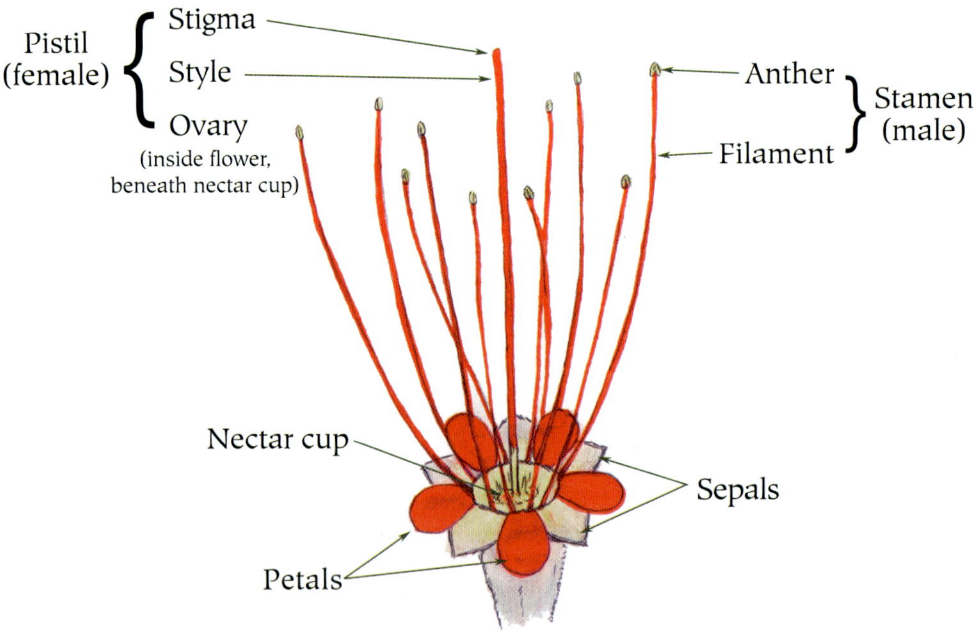

So how does pollen get transferred from one flower to another, or one tree to another, especially when individual trees may be a long way apart?

Those beautiful red blooms are not only nice for us to look at and admire, they also attract a variety of animals, including birds, bees, bats, and geckos. The animals visit the flowers to feed on the sweet nectar they produce. When an animal visits a flower, some pollen grains usually stick to its body. Then, when it visits another flower, the pollen is transferred to this flower and pollination can occur.

Inside the pollen grains are sperm cells, and inside the ovules are eggs. When a pollen grain comes into contact with a stigma, it grows a pollen tube down inside the style towards the ovules. When the pollen tube reaches an ovule, a sperm cell joins with an egg to form an embryo. This is called fertilisation. The embryo inside the ovule becomes the seed. When the seed germinates, it is the embryo inside it that grows into the new plant.

A. Arkins

Some cultivated pohutukawa have yellow and green ('variegated') leaves.

Flower colours

Most pohutukawa trees produce the familiar, deep-red flowers. However, there are some individuals that have pink, yellow, apricot, or salmon-coloured flowers. Usually these different colours can only be reproduced by taking cuttings from the tree. This is because most seeds from these unusual trees would grow into plants that have the normal red flowers.

In this picture you can see the yellow pollen on the end of the stamens.

Pohutukawa seeds that result from self-pollination often do not contain an embryo. In other words, they are not fertile seeds. This means that they will not germinate and grow. A higher proportion of fertile seeds result from cross-pollination. So it's important for the long-term survival of pohutukawa in the wild that there are enough trees and enough pollinators to ensure cross-pollination.

The pohutukawa flowers from November to January. Each flower stays open for about seven days. After this, the stamens fall to the ground, and light green seed capsules develop. Like the young leaves, the young capsules are covered in tiny, fine hairs. From summer until autumn the capsules become larger as the seeds grow inside them. The seeds are tiny, only a few millimetres long! Each capsule has about 900 seeds.

In autumn and early winter the capsules open and release the seeds. The seeds are carried on the wind and may travel for long distances, but only those that are fertile and land in a favourable spot will have a chance to grow into a healthy pohutukawa tree.

Where are the petals?

The most obvious parts of many flowers are the petals. You may have thought that there were no petals on pohutukawa flowers, but they are there — you just have to look closely, as they are very small!

The stamens of this flower have fallen off, leaving the pistils behind.

Seed capsules of a pohutukawa tree.

Evolution

The ancestors of pohutukawa and its relatives are thought to be some of the earliest flowering plants to evolve in New Zealand. *Metrosideros* species first appear in fossil records between 55 and 65 million years ago.

A team of biologists from Auckland University has recently discovered that all of the *Metrosideros* species found throughout the Pacific probably originated from New Zealand. This means that the ancestors of pohutukawa and rata first evolved in New Zealand, and then the seeds were carried on the wind to other Pacific islands, where they established and evolved into new species.

This pohutukawa leaf fossil was found in the Waikato region.

Ecology is the study of how living things interact with each other. There are many other species that live in association with pohutukawa. Some are easily seen, such as the birds and bees that pollinate the flowers. Others are less obvious, like the insects that feed on pohutukawa leaves. But they all have a role to play in the complex ecosystem they are part of.

Pohutukawa pollinators

When flowering, pohutukawa trees often become a bustling centre of activity, attracting many different animals to feed on the nectar. An average-sized tree may produce up to ten litres of nectar during a flowering season (that's five 2-litre bottles of milk!). As the animals drink the nectar from the base of the flower, pollen grains stick to their bodies, and when the animals move to flowers on another tree, cross-pollination may occur. The nectar has a high nutritional value, so both the tree and the pollinators benefit from this relationship.

Pohutukawa is one of only a few New Zealand native plants that are known to attract pollinators both day and night. During the day birds and bees make up the biggest group of visitors, and after the sun goes down bats and geckos start the night shift.

Native birds such as the tui, bellbird, and stitchbird were originally important pollinators of pohutukawa. As a group, these birds are known as 'honey-eaters' because nectar from pohutukawa and other flowers is a major part of their diet. The tips of their tongues are brush-like, which helps them to sip the nectar. The native parrot, the kaka, also visits pohutukawa flowers for nectar. Today, many of these birds are rare or absent on the mainland, and are found on only a few offshore islands. While they remain important to the life cycle of pohutukawa on these islands, on the mainland their role as pollinators has largely been taken over by introduced birds such as sparrows and starlings.

Kaka.

Most people are familiar with the introduced honeybee that produces all the honey we eat. These bees make a very good honey from pohutukawa nectar. However, many people don't know that there are also about 40 species of native bees in New Zealand. They are all

Honeybee.

solitary, which means that they live on their own and don't build hives. Along with the honeybees, they play a significant role in the pollination of pohutukawa flowers.

This small native bee is gathering pollen, which it carries on its hind legs. Unlike honeybees, native bees do not drink the nectar from the pohutukawa flower.

We have only two species of bats native to New Zealand. The long-tailed bat is thought to eat mostly insects. The short-tailed bat, on the other hand, eats nectar, fruit, pollen, spiders, centipedes and millipedes, as well as weta and other insects. Research to date shows that it has the broadest diet of almost any bat in the world! This bat needs fairly large areas of native bush to live in. Unfortunately, due to the clearing of native forest by humans, short-tailed bats are now rare in coastal areas where the pohutukawa grows. One of the best examples of the pohutukawa–bat relationship is on Little Barrier Island. Walking beneath the pohutukawa at night during the flowering season, you may

A. Arkins

Short-tailed bat covered in pollen. Scientists have caught this bat in a net as part of a research project.

hear short-tailed bats chattering and squeaking as they drink the nectar, often becoming almost completely covered in pollen in the process. The pollen is then transferred from flower to flower as the bats move around. Like the honey-eater birds, the short-tailed bat also has a brush-tipped tongue to help it sip nectar.

Tree-dwelling lizards, such as the Pacific gecko and forest gecko, have been seen feeding on pohutukawa nectar. These native lizards are

Forest gecko sipping nectar from the nectar cup at the base of a pohutukawa flower.

nocturnal, and come out at dusk to lap up nectar with their tongues. As they do this pollen rubs off onto their heads and throats, and is then carried from flower to flower as the geckos move around and between trees. These lizards are rare today on the mainland, but populations exist on some offshore islands.

A. Arkins

A small area of coastal forest that is dominated by pohutukawa.

Pohutukawa forest

The pohutukawa is the dominant tree in the few small areas of pohutukawa forest that remain. Its upper branches often form a continuous canopy shading the ground underneath, where ferns, grasses, and other shade-loving plants, such as kawakawa and hange-hange, can grow. In some places on the Poor Knights Islands, the Poor Knights lily grows in large numbers beneath the pohutukawa canopy.

Tree species like kohekohe, puriri, karaka and titoki also grow together with pohutukawa, especially further inland where the conditions are not so harsh.

Like many of our forest trees, the branches of

the pohutukawa are often laden with epiphytes. These are usually perching plants such as kahakaha. They grow from a seed which germinates on a tree branch. By living up in the branches of trees, perching plants don't have to compete with other plants on the forest floor for space and light.

This large pohutukawa tree supports many kahakaha epiphytes.

Rangitoto Island: a young forest

Rangitoto Island is a volcano that was formed about 600 years ago. When European settlers first arrived here almost 200 years ago, the island was still mostly bare lava that had cooled and solidified. Lichens and mosses grew on the rocks, plus some small trees. Many of these trees were young pohutukawa, grown from seeds that had been blown over onto the island and caught in the crevices between the rocks. When they flowered they attracted birds, which in turn carried the seeds of other plants to the island.

Today, Rangitoto Island is covered in the largest pohutukawa forest in New Zealand. Many of the trees have matured to a large size and provide a sheltering canopy under which other plants can grow. There are still areas of bare lava where you can see young pohutukawa plants growing among the rocks.

In the 1870s possums and brush-tailed rock wallabies from Australia were introduced onto Motutapu Island, which adjoins Rangitoto Island by a small land-bridge. These animals soon crossed over onto Rangitoto Island, and caused enormous damage to the pohutukawa. Some trees were so heavily browsed that they died. However, the possums and wallabies were recently eradicated from the island by the Department of Conservation.

Insect life

Insect damage on pohutukawa leaves.

Sometimes you will see pohutukawa that have many holes in their leaves. A large variety of insects make their home in pohutukawa trees, and browse on the leaves and flowers. Many of these insects are endemic to New Zealand, and have evolved a close relationship with pohutukawa. Their browsing does not usually cause much harm to the tree.

The native leaf-mining weevil causes a large proportion of pohutukawa leaf damage. The female adult weevil eats the new leaves of pohutukawa, then lays her eggs at the base of a leaf. The larvae then also eat the leaves. In response to this, the tree drops the damaged leaves. In some cases this can cause the loss of many leaves, but studies have shown that this does not usually significantly damage the health of the tree.

Birds

Saddleback.

Pohutukawa trees provide food and nesting spaces for birds. Tui, bellbirds, silvereyes and starlings are some of the birds attracted to the flower nectar. On some offshore islands, such as Little Barrier Island and Tiritiri Matangi Island in the Hauraki Gulf, the saddleback sometimes nests in holes in pohutukawa, and also searches through the rough bark for insects to eat.

Birds of the sea and shore are also associated with pohutukawa trees because they live in the same habitat. Shags and white-faced herons often make nests or roost at night in the branches of pohutukawa.

Pied shags resting in the branches of a pohutukawa tree.

THREATS TO POHUTUKAWA

Even though there are large, old pohutukawa in most northern coastal areas, these trees represent only a very small proportion of the numbers that once existed. Evidence suggests that pohutukawa originally formed large areas of forest along our northern coasts. Today, there are only a few places left where you can see a 'pohutukawa forest'. The majority of these are on islands, such as Rangitoto Island. On mainland New Zealand, many pohutukawa trees have disappeared, leaving behind the few large, old trees that we see today.

A. Arkins

There are a number of reasons for their disappearance. Maori used fire to clear the land, but the fires sometimes got out of control, and large areas of coastal pohutukawa forest were destroyed.

When European settlers first started arriving in New Zealand in the nineteenth century, they also began clearing coastal land to make way for towns and farms. Pohutukawa wood burns very well, so it was a favourite choice for firewood, and was also used for smoking fish. The natural curves in the timber made it ideal for building parts of the frames of sailing ships. Because of its attractive reddish colour, the wood was also used for furniture-making. Within a short time, pohutukawa numbers had been drastically reduced, and the future for pohutukawa didn't look too good.

Today, we don't usually cut down pohutukawa trees. In spite of this, their existence is still threatened. One reason for this is that although pohutukawa seedlings are very good at growing in dry, rocky places, they don't compete well with other plants growing nearby. They may be able to grow perched on the side of a cliff, but have great difficulty pushing up through pasture grass. Because there are farms in many coastal areas, this means that natural regeneration of pohutukawa happens very slowly, or not at all.

Very little natural pohutukawa regeneration occurs in pastoral habitats like this one.

The distance between pohutukawa trees is another threat to their regeneration. Because so many pohutukawa have been removed in the past, it is quite common to find individual trees separated from each other by long distances. This means that it is less likely that birds and other pollinators will move between the trees and cross-pollinate them. This in turn results in fewer fertile seeds, and therefore fewer new seedlings.

Fire is also a significant threat to pohutukawa. Like all other members of the myrtle family, the leaves and bark of pohutukawa burn very easily. A relatively small amount of fire damage can result in the death of a mature tree.

Some herbivorous animals are a threat to pohutukawa. Sheep and cattle will eat the leaves of pohutukawa. But the worst offender is the brush-tailed possum. Possums are not native to New Zealand — they were first brought here from Australia in the middle of the nineteenth century, and released into the forests so that people could hunt them for their fur. Possum numbers have gradually increased and they have now spread throughout most of New Zealand. The buds and leaves of pohutukawa and its forest relative, the rata, are a favourite food of the possum. In many places you can see the bare 'skeletons' of trees that have been killed by possum-browsing.

Possums were first released in New Zealand in 1858 into the forest near Riverton in the South Island. Back then nobody knew how

Possum browsing can kill mature pohutukawa trees.

Possum facts

• Scientific name: *Trichosurus vulpecula*. This is Latin for 'hairy-tailed little fox'.
• Possums are omnivores, which means that they eat a wide range of foods including leaves, flowers and buds, fruits, fungi, invertebrates, small mammals, birds and eggs.
• As well as eating native animals, possums may compete with them for food and nesting sites.
• It has been estimated that there are 70 million possums in New Zealand, and that collectively they eat about 21,000 tonnes of vegetation each night!
• Possums are native to Australia.
• Possums are marsupials. These are a group of mammals whose young are born at a very early stage. They complete their development inside the mother's pouch, where they suckle milk, like other mammals. Kangaroos and wallabies are other well-known examples of marsupials. When a young possum grows too big to fit inside its mother's pouch, it rides upon her back, clinging to her fur.
• Possums are nocturnal. This means they are mostly active at night. During the day they rest in their dens, which are usually inside hollow trees and branches, under logs, inside the roofs of buildings, or in a clump of perching plants.

much damage they would cause to our native plants and animals. Possum skins were very valuable in those days, and there was a flourishing trade in skins until the 1920s. About this time, people were becoming aware that possums were damaging our native forests, and in 1946 the use of poisons to control possum numbers was made legal. Today we know that possums are responsible for the decline of many native species. For instance, possums have been recorded on video eating the eggs of native birds such as the wood pigeon. It is highly unlikely that we will ever be able to eradicate possums from New Zealand, but in many areas conservation workers carry out regular trapping and poisoning programmes to try to keep possum numbers at a low level.

CONSERVATION

Until recently, the pohutukawa was in danger of extinction. Biologists estimate that up to 90 percent of the original pohutukawa forests were removed by fire or axe. Add to that the threats faced by pohutukawa, and you can see why the species was in trouble.

In 1990 a trust called Project Crimson was formed. Its aim is to protect pohutukawa. In 1996 the protection was extended to include tree rata, after reports that they also were declining. Project Crimson provides funds for tree planting and maintenance by community groups, iwi, and schools, and also supports scientific research projects.

Pohutukawa planted at Omana Regional Park.

Much of the trust's work involves gathering seeds and growing seedlings for planting

PROJECT CRIMSON

CarterHoltHarvey
with the Department of Conservation

Did you know?

The New Zealand pohutukawa has been introduced to South Africa as a garden plant. However, it is now classed as a weed there because some of the seeds from these garden plants have taken root in the wild.

In one particular area, thousands of pohutukawa seedlings are growing and local people are pulling out as many of them as they can. The people are worried that the pohutukawa will invade other areas and pose a threat to native South African plants.

projects. Since 1990 more than 300,000 pohutukawa and rata trees have been planted during Project Crimson activities. Recent surveys have shown that this planting, along with possum control carried out by landowners, the Department of Conservation and local councils, has resulted in a large increase in pohutukawa regeneration in some areas. These successes show that if we all work together we can make a significant difference to the health of our environment. But the work must continue if we are to ensure a bright future for pohutukawa.

Case study — Cape Brett possum fence

In 1995 the building of an electric possum-proof fence across the Cape Brett Peninsula in Northland was completed. The fence is 2.5 km long, solar-powered, and prevents possums from crossing over onto the peninsula, which is home to many large, old pohutukawa trees.

Project Crimson, the Department of Conservation, the Northland Regional Council and local Maori landowners joined together to build the fence after reports of severe damage to pohutukawa on the peninsula by possums.

Since the completion of the fence, some pohutukawa trees have flowered for the first time in many years. The possum population on the peninsula has been significantly reduced by a trapping and poisoning programme, and the fence prevents most possums from reinvading the area from outside the fence.

You can see the fence if you walk along the Cape Brett track. This is an eight-hour tramping track that finishes at the hut at the end of the peninsula. The Department of Conservation office in Russell has maps and details.

What can you do to help?

There are many ways that you can contribute to the future of pohutukawa. It's important to remember that doing even small things can make a difference. Planting trees is a good start, even if you only plant one pohutukawa in your garden! By doing this you will also be providing a food source for nectar-eating birds, encouraging them back into our towns and cities.

You could get involved with a local planting programme, or ask your school or community group to consider starting up a pohutukawa nursery or planting project. Possum control is also very important, and your local council should be able to give you advice about the best way to do this.

Glossary

browse to search for and eat leaves and other vegetation.

colonise to become established in a new environment.

ecosystem all the living and non-living things in a defined area and the relationships between them.

endemic describes an organism that does not occur naturally anywhere else on earth.

epiphyte a plant that grows on another plant, but is not a parasite.

eradicate to completely remove a species from an area.

fertilisation the union of sperm and egg to form an embryo.

germinate for a seed to sprout and grow.

herbivore/herbivorous an animal that eats only plants.

hermaphrodite having both male and female reproductive parts.

marsupial type of mammal whose young are born very young and helpless, and complete their development inside the mother's pouch.

nectar sweet, sugary fluid produced by flowers to attract insects, birds and other animals which pollinate the flowers.

nocturnal active at night.

omnivore an animal that eats both plants and other animals.

ovule female part of a flower that contains the egg, and grows into a seed after fertilisation.

pistil all the female parts of a flower.

pollen tiny grains produced by the male flower parts for reproduction.

pollen tube tube produced by a pollen grain when it contacts a stigma; grows down the style to the ovary to allow sperm cells to reach the ovules.

pollination the transfer of pollen from the male to the female parts of a flower.

regeneration in this context, means the establishment of new seedlings to replace dead and dying trees.

stamen the male parts of a flower.

Index